Day Hiking Trails of
Washburn
County

I0115717

By Rob Bignell

Atiswinic Press · Ojai, Calif.

DAY HIKING TRAILS OF WASHBURN COUNTY

A GUIDEBOOK IN THE
HITTIN' THE TRAIL: WISCONSIN SERIES

Copyright Rob Bignell, 2017

Atiswinic Press
Ojai, Calif. 93023
dayhikingtrails.wordpress.com

ISBN 978-0-9961625-7-9

Cover design by Rob Bignell
Cover photo: A young porcupine, common in Washburn County, explores
the base of a tree in springtime.
All interior photos by Rob Bignell

Manufactured in the United States of America
First printing April 2017

For Kieran
"Now he walks in quiet solitude the forest and the streams/Seeking grace in every step he takes" – John Denver

Contents

Introduction

I magine a place where sun-dappled paths run alongside murmuring rivers, where trails retrace former rail lines past historic depots, where real carnivorous plants line your walking route, where a mile-high glacier shaped the hummocky forests around you, where any turn of the corner might reveal a majestic white-tailed buck or a tiny young porcupine sunning itself upon a rock, where bald eagles and osprey regally circle and swoop high above the trees. The place is real: It's called Washburn County, Wisconsin.

Located in Wisconsin's northwest corner, Washburn County is an outdoor recreational paradise. During summers, bicyclists and off-road vehicle enthusiasts ply a number of wooded trails while fishermen and canoeists try their hand at their sport on freshwater lakes and a nationally protected riverway. Come autumn, the roads turn busy with drivers out to enjoy the colorful blaze of autumn leaves. Throughout winter, cross-country skiers, snowshoers and snowmobilists sail across white paths while ice fishing shacks pop up on frozen lakes.

And, of course, day and backcountry hikers alike enjoy the county's hundreds of miles of trails, some routes well-groomed and others primitive, but all rambling through verdant scenery.

Geology

Two lengthy geological events shaped Washburn County's terrain: the erosion of a vast, ancient mountain range; and the ice ages of the past million years.

About 600-700 million years ago, the northern third of the county was part of a great Alps-like mountain range. Most of what is now central and southern Wisconsin lay under an ocean.

Over the eons, streams and rivers carried sediment out of these mountains, filling the shallow sea inch by inch. The sandstone found in road cuts and on river banks across the southern part of the county and Wisconsin as a whole are those piles of sediment.

Erosion has worn those mountains down into a relatively flat area, with occasional hills, called a peneplain.

Then, glaciers during the last ice age brought sediment – mainly sand, gravel and boulder clay – that was left across the base of those ancient mountains and the filled-in sea. Because of this, the northern part of the county generally is better for forests than farming, which in our century shapes up to great hiking trails.

The southern two-thirds of the county is largely shaped by the ice age as well. As the glaciers melted and retreated at the end of the last ice age, they left long narrow mounds of sediment called hummocks. Ice-walled lakes also formed, leaving whole swaths of land fairly flat.

The county's central hilly area – known as the Spooner Hills – were created by till piling up during several glacial advances. The spacing between the hills likely developed when melting ice at the glacier's bottom formed tunnels so that the water flowed outward into the open plain to the south.

Geography

The county consists of two distinct geographical regions.

The southern portion – including Shell Lake and Birchwood – as well as much of the county's northeast quarter, largely consists of highlands, sitting at an elevation of 1200-

1400 feet. While not significant compared to the Appalachians or the Rockies, for Wisconsin, this is a good 200-400 feet higher than much of the southern part of the state. This forested region sports a great diversity of trees that typically can be found across the state.

The county's center, including Spooner, Trego and Minong, sits at a lower 1000-1200 feet elevation. This is the dried, sandy bed of Glacial Lake Grantsburg, which existed near the end of the last Ice Age when a glacier in Minnesota dammed the flow of meltwater. Some of the county's northwest quadrant, which is closer to the center of the extinct lake, is at an even lower elevation of 800-1200 feet. The sandier soil tends to nurture forests of pine, aspen-birch and oak. Today, the Namekagon River flows through this county's center.

Communities

Several great hiking trails crisscross Washburn County, with many of them centered on five major communities. Adding to the county's charm is that no community has a population of more than 3000, and only one town even comes close to that.

The village of Birchwood sits tucked in the county's southeast corner on Wis. Hwy. 48. The self-proclaimed Bluegill Capital of Wisconsin, it's a former 1800s logging camp that became a town in its own right. The Tuscobia State Trail runs through it.

Washburn's county seat, Shell Lake, is in the opposite corner along U.S. Hwy. 63. The town is centered on its namesake, popular Shell Lake, so named because shells of freshwater bivalves were common on its lakeshore. Several hiking trails can be found in or near town, including the Ice Age National Scenic Trail.

Just north of Shell Lake where U.S. Hwys. 63 and 53 join

and split, is Spooner, the county's largest city. Nicknamed "Crossroads of the North," at one time it was a hub of the Omaha Railroad Line. A former rail line, the Wild Rivers State Trail is now a hiking/bicycling path running south to Sarona and Rice Lake and north to Trego and Superior.

Unincorporated Trego can be found at the county's center on the Namekagon River in the St. Croix National Scenic Riverway. Hwy. 63 goes east here to Hayward while Hwy. 53 goes north to Superior. The former heads to the scenic riverway's visitor center and the picturesque Trego Nature Trail.

The village of Minong is in the northcentral portion of the county along Hwy. 53 at the edge of Wisconsin's northern highlands. The Wild Rivers State Trail runs through town while the Totagatic Ski Trail loops are nearby.

Attractions

Three major attractions stand out for day and backcountry hikers in Washburn County. Across much of the county's southern section, the 1200-mile **Ice Age National Scenic Trail** winds its way toward its western and northern terminus, loosely marking the edge of where glaciers once stood more than 10,000 years ago during the last ice age. Cutting north to south through the county is the **Wild Rivers State Trail**, which follows an abandoned rail line between the city of Rice Lake to the south and the port city of Superior to the north. Finally, splitting the county almost in half, the **St. Croix National Scenic Riverway** curves from the Namekagon's headwaters to the northeast toward a meeting with the great St. Croix River to the west.

When to Visit

The best months to day hike Washburn County are May through September. Depending on the year, April and October also can be pleasant.

As with the rest of Wisconsin, summers are humid, especially July and August. Rain can occur during the afternoon
even when the morning is sunny, so always check the weather forecast before heading out.

November through March usually is too cold for day
hiking. Once snow falls, trails typically are used for cross-
country skiing, snowmobiling or snowshoeing. Early spring
often means muddy trails thanks to snowmelt and rainfall.

How to Get There

Several major highways offer access to Washburn County.

From the Minneapolis-St. Paul area, take Interstate 94 east
into Wisconsin. At Baldwin, exit onto U.S. Hwy 63 and travel
north to Shell Lake. Those living in the northern Twin Cities
alternately can cross the Stillwater bridge and take Wis. Hwy.
64 east then turn north onto Hwy. 63. Another option is to
take Interstate 35 north, exiting in Forest Lake onto U.S. Hwy.
8, which can be taken east into Wisconsin; in Turtle Lake,
turn north onto Hwy. 63.

From northern Minnesota, at Duluth cross the Interstate
535 bridge into Wisconsin. Go south onto U.S. Hwy. 53, which
heads to Minong and cuts north-south through Washburn
County.

From western Wisconsin, take either Hwy. 63 or Hwy. 53
north into the county. The former works well for those living
along or near the Minnesota border while the latter is best
for those living near Eau Claire.

From eastern Wisconsin and the Upper Peninsula, U.S.
Hwy. 10, Wis. Hwy. 29 and Hwy. 8 each heads west, intersect-
ing either Hwy. 53 (in the case of Hwys. 29 and 8) or Hwy. 63
(as is the case with Hwys. 10, 29 and 8). Head north on Hwy.
53 or 63.

From central and southern Wisconsin, take either I-94 or
Interstate 39 north. I-94 intersects northbound Hwy. 53 in

Eau Claire. I-39 junctions Hwy. 29 in Wausau; take the latter west then turn north onto Hwy. 53 near Eau Claire/Chippewa Falls.

Maps

To properly prepare for any hike, you should examine maps before hitting the trail and bring them with you (See the Bonus Section for more.). No guidebook can reproduce a map as well as the satellite pictures or topographical maps that you can find online for free. To that end, a companion website to this book offers a variety of printable maps for each listed trail at *dayhikingtrails.wordpress.com/trail-maps*.

Featured Trails

Washburn County can loosely be divided into three sections, each with its own distinct feel. The southern third of the county, roughly below the west/east-running County Road B and the Stone Lake area, marks **Southern Lake Country**. It sports a number of kettle lakes, left here by glaciers during the most recent ice age. The county's largest lakes – Shell Lake, Long Lake and Balsam Lake (which is part of the Lake Chetac-Red Cedar Lake chain) all can be found here. **Yellow River Country** is centered on its namesake river, which runs through the county's center at Spooner heading west. **Namekagon River Country** begins near the river's shore and includes the entire north of the county, which is classic Wisconsin Northwoods.

Southern Lake Country

Known for its excellent fishing lakes, the county's southern portion, from roughly Shell Lake to Stone Lake, offers a great variety of forest types, including maple-basswood, pine groves, white-red oak highlands, and low-lying birch-aspen. It makes for excellent hiking country.

Ice Age National Scenic Trail, Grassy Lake segment

South of Shell Lake, a fairly flat segment of the expansive Ice Age National Scenic Trail runs at the edge of where the glacier last seen in these parts towered some 11,000 years ago. The hike to Grassy Lake and back makes for just under 4 miles round trip.

To reach the trail, from Shell Lake drive south on U.S. Hwy. 63. At Brick Yard Road, go left/east. At the next intersection, turn right/south onto Old Hwy. 63; park off this road across from the Pershing Road intersection.

The trail unofficially heads east alongside Pershing Road. You'll pass bucolic farm fields at first, but the trail grows increasingly forested as heading east. Typical Northern hardwoods – maples and oaks – with scattered pines line the route.

At about 0.75 miles, the trail turns left/north. This now official segment of the Ice Age Trail runs on public land. If you feel uncomfortable leaving your car along the highway or want to shorten your walk, this is a good alternative for parking (though it'll still have to be off the road).

A mere 11 millennia ago, this area was beneath a towering glacier, only miles away from its leading edge to the south. The glacier crushed and flattened the landscape, and remnants of it formed many of the lakes seen across northern Wisconsin by depressing the land and melting.

For the next 1.25 miles, the trail roughly parallels the shoreline of Grassy Lake, though you're never closer than 200 feet to it. The lake covers 38 acres.

The trail soon curves east, briefly paralleling the Grassy Lake's north shore. When the trail swerves north again, you've reached the turn-back point.

Upon reaching 65th Avenue, you've gone 1.5 miles. This marks a good spot to head back.

Bear Trail
Hunt Hill Audubon Sanctuary

Carnivorous plants and glacial lakes await hikers at the Hunt Hill Audubon Sanctuary east of Shell Lake.

Perhaps the best way to see the sanctuary's wide variety of ecosystems is the Bear Trail, a 2.7-mile loop to which this recommended hike adds a half-mile. Owned by the National Audubon Society, the nonprofit Friends of Hunt Hill Audubon Sanctuary operates the facility, where they offer several quality educational programs.

Trails are open from dusk to dawn. Unlike state parks, entry is free for hiking. If able, though, help fill the donation boxes on the information kiosks. Late June marks a good time to visit because of the blooming orchids, but days can get humid and insect repellent is encouraged.

To reach the sanctuary, from U.S. Hwy. 53 between Sarona/Shell Lake and Spooner take County Road B east. Turn right/south on County Road M then turn left/northwest onto Audubon Road. In about a mile, turn right/north on Hunt Hill Road. Go right/east at first intersection and park at the cluster of buildings.

Continue walking east on the road that you parked your vehicle. At the end is the Vole Trail loop; go left on the loop. To the south is a prairie where wildflowers abound in summer. You'll find the fairly even trail remains flat the rest of the way.

Sphagnum bog

Next you'll pass a sphagnum bog that borders Upper and Lower Twin Lakes. Unlike swamps, sphagnum bogs don't stink because of the water's high acidity.

In about a quarter of a mile, will come to the Bog Board-walk, a 0.1-mile loop that takes you into the wetlands where you can see two carnivorous plants – the pitcher and the sundew. Such plants usually can be found in bogs and rock outcroppings, where the soil is nutrient poor, and make up the difference by eating insects.

A number of plants live in the sphagnum bog; most notably, in late June showy orchids bloom. Other plants you'll find here include the arethusa, grass pink, pink lady's slipper, rose pogonia, sphagnum moss, and tamarack.

Continuing on the Vole Trail, you'll parallel Lower Twin Lake. From here on out, the trail is heavily forested with mixed hardwoods and pines, providing pleasant shade on hot days.

The Twin Lakes formed some 10,000 years ago when a retreating glacier's chunk broke off. As sediment deposited around the melting ice, the lakes formed. Upper Twin Lake reaches an impressive depth of 53 feet.

Upon reaching Heron Point, the trail turns south. At the T-intersection, go left/northeast onto Bear Trail. You'll cross an old WCC footbridge over a beaver pond.

Watch for 240 birds

The trail then curves past Lower Twin Lake's southern-most edge and another bog. As you turn northeast, a small quarter mile loop – the Log Road Trail – comes off and re-joins Bear Trail. This loop can be skipped.

As nearing Reed Lake, the trail curves northwest. Keep an

eye out for osprey; a platform for the hunting bird sits on opposite shore.

If a bird watcher, Hunt Hill is the place to be. Up to 240 species of birds have been spotted here. They include bald eagles, bluebirds, bobolinks, chickadees, the common loon, the Eastern meadowlark, the great egret, the green-backed heron, pheasant, the pileated woodpecker, the red owl, the red-shouldered hawk, the rose-breasted grosbeak, ruffed grouse, the sandhill crane, tree swallows, the veery, warblers, wild turkey, wood ducks, and wrens.

Leaving Reed Lake, you'll pass a bog between it and Big Devil's Lake. The trail then curves back toward Upper Twin Lake. The rise of land in the middle of the wetlands next to Lower Twin Lake is Osprey Isle, where there's another osprey platform.

Mammals and footbridge

The trail then jags in the opposite direction toward Big Devil's Lake. The 0.1-mile Big Devil's Lake Trail loops off the main route for a close up of the waterbody and also can be skipped.

Common Northwoods mammals are likely to be seen on the Bear Trail. Whitetail deer, raccoons, squirrels and chipmunks abound. There's a bear's den nearby. Watch the trees for bite marks and girdling, a sign of porcupines.

Following the Big Devil's Lake shoreline for a while, the trail soon reaches Nordskog Footbridge at Wet Crossing. Take the new footbridge over a channel that connects Big Devil's Lake to Upper Twin Lake; before the bridge, hikers had to wade through the knee-deep stream.

The trail then skirts another bog next to Upper Twin Lake until coming to the Francis Andrews Trail. Go left onto the Francis Andrews back to the main cluster of buildings and your vehicle.

Tuscobia Trail

Wisconsin has nicely converted a number of abandoned railroad grades to hiking and multi-use trails. Among the more popular is the 74-mile Tuscobia State Trail running from Rice Lake to Park Falls.

In the southeast corner of Washburn County, the trail passes through the village of Birchwood, the self-proclaimed Bluegill Capital of Wisconsin. A pleasant segment of the trail to day hike goes northeast from downtown Birchwood for a 4-mile round trip to County Road F and back.

Birchwood east segment

Hiking the trail anytime in summer and autumn will prove enjoyable. Note that the trail closes from Nov. 15-Dec. 15 for deer hunting season.

To reach the trail segment, park downtown, picking up the Tuscobia on County Road D/Euclid Avenue just north of the Wis. Hwy. 48 intersection.

After walking just a tenth of a mile, hikers will come to the south end of Birchwood Lake. The popular fishing lake covers 364 acres and is home to largemouth and smallmouth bass, Northern pike, walleye and panfish.

Passing the lake, the trail swerves to the south side of Hwy. 48; be careful when crossing the highway, especially of vehicles turning off La Pointe Drive onto Hwy. 48 a few feet to the east. ATVs also can use the trail, and while it's plenty wide for both vehicle and hiker, always exercise caution.

A project since 1968

Construction of the Omaha rail line that is now the Tuscobia begin in 1899 and lasted for some 15 years. By the 1940s when logging was no longer viable in the region, the rail line saw much less usage, which eventually ended altogether. Wooden bridges over some waterways were torn out

Tuscobia State Trail at Birchwood

in 1967, and the following year locals across the region began a long, concerted effort to convert it to a hiking trail.

Upon leaving town, the trail passes scenic farmland. Trees line the walking path, offering some shade.

Amid the scenery, you'll cross an unmarked boundary into Sawyer County then enter a bucolic woods of mixed hardwoods.

Upon reaching County Road F, you've gone 2 miles one way. This marks a good spot to turn around, though the trail does continue for several more miles on its way to Couderay.

Other Southern Lake Country Trails

• **Red Oak East and West trails** – Located at the Hunt Hill Audubon Sanctuary, combine the two looping trails for a 1.8-mile hike. Despite the trails' names, the highlight is a grove of large white pines that have been growing since the 1800s.

• **Ridge Walking Trails** – In Stone Lake, these trails ram-

Sawyer Brook Springs Trail in Shell Lake

ble through the 17.4-acre Stone Lake Wetland Park. The park also offers a 600-foot boardwalk and covered walking bridge.

• **Sawyer Brook Springs trails** – A set of three loops, primarily maintained as cross-country ski trails, begin behind the Shell Lake Arts Center in Shell Lake. The Yellow loop takes hikers twice across Sawyer Brook Springs.

• **South Side Walking Trail** – This comfortable path of wood chips works its way through meadows and wooded areas. The trail begins off of U.S. Hwy. 63 on Shell Lake's south side.

• **Wild Rivers State Trail, Sarona segment** – This three-county trail runs along a former train route through Sarona on its way north from Barron County. Take the trail north to Spooner's Railroad Memories Museum.

Yellow River Country

Sitting a couple of hundred feet lower in elevation than the county's southern portion, recreation here is focused on the Yellow River and Spooner Lake, which it drains. Beaver Brook Wildlife Area and the Wild Rivers State Trail – which helps preserve the area's railroad heritage – are its two major hiking centers.

Beaver Brook East Trail
Beaver Brook Wildlife Area

Day hikers can enjoy a pleasant walk along a classic trout stream on Beaver Brook Wildlife Area's East Trail. Along the way, you may spot the impressive osprey or bald eagle.

The wildlife area nicely preserves 1,964 acres of woods and wetlands between Shell Lake and Spooner. A number of loops run off the main trail so hikers can adjust the trail's length to meet their time restrictions and energy levels. Dogs also are allowed on the trail.

The wildlife area boasts multiple access points. To reach the East Trail, from Spooner head south on U.S. Hwy. 53. Turn south onto Cranberry Drive. After about a mile, just before road curves SE away from Beaver Brook, turn right into the parking lot. This places you at about the wildlife area's center.

Spring-pond fed stream

From the parking lot's northeast corner, head north paralleling Cranberry Drive then veer away from the road for a half mile to trail junction B. A 0.8-mile trail loops off here; it rejoins the main trail at junction C.

Most of the trail runs beneath mixed hardwoods, such as maple, oak and aspen. There's some conifer, pine and tamarack as well with a few red oak stands.

Continuing ahead on the main trail, you'll follow Beaver Brook for a half mile to trail junction D. There, you can get a close look at the stream in a 0.4-mile loop that rejoins the main trail at junction E. Beaver Brook stands out as a Class I brook and brown trout stream. Well-shaded – the brook doesn't show up on satellite photos – 10 spring ponds and a number of bank seeps feed it as it heads north into the Yellow River Flowage.

If you skip this loop, the distance between trail junctions D and E is 0.2 miles. At trail junction E, you'll pass the brook's largest spring pond on the trail's left side.

Dive fishing

Keep an eye out for a number of birds, who either appreciate the wooded cover or the brook's fish. Among the former are the American woodcock, ruffed grouse, and various waterfowl. Among the latter are bald eagles and the North American osprey.

Osprey can reach up to two feet in length with a wingspan of more than five feet. They feed on pan and sucker fish, and if lucky, you may see it dive for one. Osprey typically fly their search patterns some 30-100 feet above the stream and upon spotting prey dive feet first into the water. Once a fish is caught, their feet juggle it around until the prey's head faces the wind. They then take it to their perch and feed.

Beyond birds, white-tailed deer, squirrels and chipmunks are ubiquitous here.

After walking 0.75 miles, you'll come to trail junction G and another loop with a variety of options. Going right means you'll walk roughly northeast back toward Hwy. 53 for 0.68 miles. You'll hear a small amount of freeway noise, but it's momentary, as you curve away from it.

At trail junction I, you can either:

• Go left for 0.43 miles to trail junction H; from there, go

Beaver Brook East Trail

left for 0.06 miles back to trail junction G and return the way you came.

• Continue straight, looping about 1.12 miles to trail junction G (you'll pass trail junction H along the way), and then return the parking lot the way you came.

In the winter, these are ski trails with specific rules about which direction you should go on each loop. These directions aren't particularly relevant for day hikers, though.

Before heading onto the trail, you may want to stop at a local bookstore and pick up Spooner author Peter Hubin's "A Brook Runs Through It." His novel is set along Beaver Brook.

Wild Rivers State Trail, Spooner segment

Day hikers can learn about railroading on an old rail line turned hiking trail in Spooner.

The Wild Rivers State Trail runs for 104 miles across three counties on a former Omaha and Soo Line Railroads rail line. The trail connects Rice Lake in the south with Superior to the northwest.

In Spooner, the trail marks the eastern edge of downtown. A 1.9-mile round trip segment of the trail makes for a pleasant urban hike.

Start at the city's Railroad Memories Museum on Front Street. Parking is free, but admission is charged for the museum.

The museum is located in a former Chicago & Northwestern Railway depot. Between the depot, and the parked train cars, and the locomotives are 12 different rooms that hikers can go through to explore the area's rich railroad history.

At one time, Spooner was major railroad hub as lines for the Omaha and Soo Line Railroads and the Chicago & Northwestern Railway met in town. Passenger service existed until the early 1960s.

From the museum, head south on the trail. There's one major road crossing, of Wis. Hwy. 70, as the trail leaves the downtown area.

The trail next crosses the Yellow River flowage. The river is so named because of the bright yellow sand at the bottom of the lake it flows through. Today, the flowage, created to

The Wild Rivers State Trail passes historic railroad cars and a depot turned museum in Spooner.

prevent flooding, covers about 85 acres and is a prime fishing destination. More shoreline of the flowage appears on the right/west a couple of blocks up the trail.

As the Wild Rivers approaches Lois Lane, Randall Lake comes into view. A bit smaller than the flowage at 40 acres, it's also not quite as deep but still as scenic. Northern pike are common in the lake.

As Randall Lake fades in the distance, the route comes to an intersection with a spur line. This marks a good spot to turn back. Alternately, you can continue on for a 3.8-mile one-way walk to the Beaver Brook Wildlife Area.

• **Also see:** Wild Rivers State Trail in Rice Lake, Sarona, Trego and Minong

Other Yellow River Country Trails

• **College Street City Park Trail** – Several loops run through Spooner City Park at the end of College Street. One route encircles the park.

• **Nordic Woods Ski Trail** – From County Board B at the north tip of Long Lake, follow the entry trail to the A Loop for

College Street City Park Trail in Spooner

a 2.7-mile excursion. Shadow Lake is a short walk away on another loop.

Namekagon River Country

For most travelers, the Namekagon River – protected by the St. Croix National Scenic Riverway – marks the start of the Wisconsin northwoods. The riverway offers a range of outdoors opportunities, especially fishing and camping. Pines and oaks dominate much of the ecosystem heading north through Minong.

Trego Lake Trail
St. Croix National Scenic Riverway

A pretty hike through a Northwoods forest awaits hikers on the Trego Lake Trail.

The 1.9-mile trail loops through the woods next to Trego Lake. Both the lake and the trail are part of the St. Croix National Scenic Riverway.

Also known as the Trego Lake Ski Touring Trail, the path described here is a segment of its various routes. Up to 3.5 miles of trails are groomed for cross country skiing in winter.

To reach the trail, drive north of Trego on U.S. Hwy. 53. Go left/west on North River Road. In two miles, turn left/south into a parking lot. Take the stem trail from the lot's southern side to the main trail, where you'll go left/east.

The trail parallels North River Road but is nicely set inside the woodline. In autumn, the trail is comely with the yellow of birch trees leaves and orange and browns of various oaks amid the mixed hardwood and pine forest. You stand a good chance of spotting white-tailed deer and ruffed grouse in the woods.

Gradually, the trail curves south then hairpins west as coming to Trego Lake. The 383-acre waterbody actually is a widening of the Namekagon River. As such, the lake isn't particularly deep, reaching a maximum depth of just 36 feet.

About half of the trail follows the shoreline, including go-

Trego Lake Trail in the St. Croix National Scenic Riverway

ing onto a small peninsula. You're likely to see fishermen on the lake, as they try to land muskie (Wisconsin's state fish), bass (both largemouth and smallmouth flourish here), walleye, and various panfish. Northern pike and sturgeon also inhabit the lake.

After going beneath a powerline, the trail curves north,

then as nearing the road, parallels it as turning east and passing under the powerline again. Upon reaching the stem trail, go left/north back to the parking lot.

Since the trail described here is the outer loop of the ski trails, you can shorten the walk. After hiking a brief section of the shoreline, a trail goes right/north and cuts across the woods to the parking lot. This shorter route totals 1.2 miles.

You also can extend it. After veering north away from the lake, take the next trail going right/northeast; this loops over hilly terrain and rejoins the trail proper, adding about a mile to the route for a 2.9-mile round trip. Upon rejoining the trail, go right/north back to the parking lot.

Dogs are welcomed on the trail, and restrooms can be found at the trailhead.

Trego Nature Trail
St. Croix National Scenic Riverway

A pleasant walk through the woods along a wild river await hikers on the Trego Nature Trail in the St. Croix National Scenic Riverway.

The trail is best done during summer when the shaded walk keeps hikers cool. Early autumn is a good time for those who enjoy fall colors.

To reach the trail, take U.S. Hwy. 63 north of Trego village. About 1.3 miles from visitor center and after crossing the bridge over the Namekagon River, take the first right. The parking lot is at end of this entrance road.

Look for the trailhead on the parking lot's east side. The trail is fairly well-maintained. Watch for some steep inclines and narrow sections on curves, however.

The trail parallels the Namekagon River through a woods of pine and deciduous trees, with views of the waterway. Benches typically sit in the openings.

Hikers are likely to see a variety of wildlife or at least

Trego Nature Trail overlooking the Namekagon River

signs of it. White-tailed deer, turtles, fox, muskrat, bobcats, squirrels, snowshoe hares, and great blue heron abound in the riverway. Watch for otters and their slides, muddy paths cleared in the river's bank in which they move from land to water.

You also might spot lake sturgeon—Wisconsin's largest fish—especially if the water is low. They like to lay motionless beneath overhanging trees. In fact, the river's name comes from the Ojibwe Indian words that loosely mean "place of the sturgeon." Most of the sturgeon, however, is downriver below the Trego Dam.

After the footbridge, the trail loops back upon itself. Hikers can return to the parking lot the same way they came in. The trail comes to about the 2.8-miles round trip.

Dogs are allowed on the trail if leashed. For safety, don't climb the river banks as they can be slick. On the drive back home, stop at the Namekagon Visitor Center for displays about the riverway.

Wild Rivers State Trail, Trego segment
St. Croix National Scenic Riverway

A pleasant stroll through the woods with a bridge view of the Namekagon River awaits day hikers on a segment of the Wild Rivers State Trail in Trego.

At a little under 2.2-miles round trip, the segment is just a small portion of a trail that runs for 104 miles across three counties on an old Omaha and Soo Line Railroads rail line. The trail connects Rice Lake in the south with Superior to the northwest.

To pick up the trail in Trego, when U.S. Hwy. 53 enters the village from the south, turn right/east onto Oak Hill Road. Turn left/north onto Park Street. Once Park Street curves west, you'll notice a large open gravel parking lot. Leave your vehicle there. The trail runs alongside the lot's eastern side.

Take the trail northeast. Nicely forested with typical northern hardwoods, the trail is fairly isolated from built-up areas.

This section of the trail also is part of the Ice Age National Scenic Trail. The 1200-mile Ice Age Trail essentially follows the edge of where the glacier last seen in these parts towered some 10,000 years ago.

In about a quarter mile, the trail begins to skirt the back-side of the Namekagon Visitor Center grounds, which offers displays about the riverway. Unfortunately, there's no path leading from the Wild Rivers State Trail to the center; when done with the hike, consider a drive to it (take Hwy. 53 north and turn right onto U.S. Hwy. 63), especially if children are with you.

The trail then crosses busy Hwy. 63 and in another 100 feet traverses the Namekagon. From the river bridge looking west, the Namekagon breaks into a couple of back channels.

From the river, the trail re-enters the peaceful woods.

The Wild Rivers State Trail crosses the Namekagon River.

You're likely to spot white-tailed deer, rabbits, squirrels and chipmunks along the way. Songbirds are plentiful, providing a sweet soundtrack to the hike. In 0.75 miles, the trail reaches Ross Road, which is a good spot to turn back; by this point, you've actually left the scenic riverway.

During spring and early summer, be sure to carry insect repellant when near the river. And while the trail cuts through woodlands, it is wide and mostly open, so be also sure to don sunscreen.

Totagatic Ski Trail, Loop A

Multiple ski loop trails in winter serve as great day hiking paths in summer for those in the Minong area.

Of the four Totagatic Ski Trail loops, try Loop A. At two miles round trip, it's the shortest as well as the closest to the parking lot so is easy to locate.

To reach the trail system, head a little more than a mile

north of Minong village on U.S. Hwy. 53. At the second, or northernmost, intersection with Lakeside Road, turn left/ east into the parking lot.

A jeep trail runs west from the parking lot for 0.25 miles. Most of the trail is mixed hardwoods, consisting of sugar and red maple and basswood. On other loops, trails head through groves of replanted trees.

At the first divide in trail, head straight (or left/ west) to do the route clockwise. You're now officially on Loop A.

The trails run through a border area between two eco-systems – the North Central Forest and the Northwest Sands regions. The major difference is the former's soil is only 5-10 feet above the bedrock while the latter can have a separation of several hundred feet. In part because of this, the North Central Forest is better able to hold hardwood trees such as maples whereas the Northwest Sands is pine and shrubland.

In 0.25 miles, the trail comes to a junction. Go right/north on a section of trail shared with Loop B.

The North Central Forest covers a lot of territory in Wisconsin; it can be found in 19 counties and stretches into Michigan's Upper Peninsula. Often when thinking of the "Northwoods," an image of the North Central Forest is what comes to mind for most Wisconsinites and travelers.

The next trail junction comes in about 0.1 miles; at it, go right/north. The trail you didn't take heads onto Loop B, which in turn connects with loops C and D.

"Totagatic" is derived from the Ojibwa word "Totogan," which means "boggy river." The trails, however, don't go near their namesake river, which is to the north by a few miles. In any case, the Native Americans' name for the area that includes Minong village and these ski trails translates to "Pleasant Valley."

After about 0.25 miles, Loop A veers east and gradually curves south. In little more than 0.9 miles, you'll reach the

Totagatic Ski Trail

access trail that leads to the parking lot; go left/east back to the lot.

Other Namekagon Country Trails

• **Leisure Lake Trail** – Northwest of Trego, a 3-mile trail heads about Leisure Lake, off of Skunk Lake Road. The lake's shoreline is nicely forested.

• **Totagatic River State Wildlife Area Jeep Trail (off**

Wozny Road – Park at the trailhead off the southeast side of Wozny Road about 800 feet north of the Totagatic River bridge. A jeep trail heads between a forested area and the Totagatic Flowage in the wildlife area's northwest corner for about 1.1 miles one-way (2.2-miles round trip).

• **Wild Rivers State Trail, Minong segment** – The former rail line turned hiking trail heads through Minong on the way from Trego to Gordon. Starting at South Limits Road, head south on the trail to Lakeside Lake for a roughly 4-mile round trip.

Neighboring Counties

T he six counties surrounding Washburn County offer plenty of great hiking opportunities that are easy for anyone staying in Spooner-Shell Lake-Trego-Minong to reach. To the north is **Douglas County**, a largely forested area with Lake Superior beaches. Going clockwise, next is **Bayfield County**; though Washburn shares only a corner point with Bayfield, it's worth the visit given the vast Chequamegon State Forest. To the east is **Sawyer County**, where the popular Northwoods destination of Hayward sits. Washburn's southeast corner touches Rusk County, well known for its ancient Blue Hills recreational area. Along Washburn's southern border is **Barron County**; most Washburn County visitors will have to pass through it on either U.S. Hwys. 53 or 63 to reach Shell Lake or Spooner. Finally, to the west is **Burnett County**, which is cabin country for many Twin Cities and Wisconsin residents.

Douglas County

From Minong, U.S. Hwy. 53 heads directly into Douglas County and offers access to more of the St. Croix National Scenic Riverway. Among the most dramatic portions of the St. Croix is its headwaters area, which sit just outside the scenic riverway.

Gordon Flowage Campground Trail
Gordon Dam County Park

Day hikers can explore the northernmost reaches of the St. Croix National Scenic Riverway on the Gordon Flowage Campground Trail.

The roughly 2-mile round trip is a jeep trail running through the woods bordering the river. The trail actually is unnamed, but for convenience's sake, we've christened it here after the campground where it begins in Gordon Dam County Park.

To reach the trailhead, from U.S. Hwy. 53 in Gordon, go west on County Road Y. Within a half-mile, you'll see a lake on your right/north. That's the Saint Croix Flowage. After about seven miles, the road dead ends. This is the northern end of the St. Croix National Scenic Riverway. Park in the Gordon Flowage Campground lot at the end of the county road.

Begin the hike by walking to the dam that creates the flowage about 300 feet northeast of the lot. The river is left/west of the dam with the 2247-acre flowage to the right/east.

The flowage – a man-made lake to prevent river flooding – reaches 28 feet deep and is popular among fishermen. Large-mouth bass, northern pike, and panfish are fairly abundant in the moderately clear water. Sometimes referred to as the Gordon-Saint Croix Flowage, it boasts 29 miles of meandering shoreline.

The flowage isn't the St. Croix River's headwaters. The river rushes into the lake's east end near Gordon after roughly paralleling Hwy. 53 from Upper St. Croix Lake near Solon Springs. Centuries ago, European explorers and fur traders portaged from Upper St. Croix Lake to the Brule River, which flows into Lake Superior, using this route to reach the Mississippi River.

From the dam, head back to the parking lot and pick up the jeep trail at the end of County Road Y. The trail heads west, with a brief jog south, through a mixed hardwood and pine forest. It's a lovely walk during autumn with the leaves alight in reds, oranges, yellows and the pine needles' dark greens. You won't see the river from the trail, but you'll likely hear it flowing over the dam.

In about 0.95 miles, the trail junctions with the asphalt Mail Road (Some maps label it as "West Mail Road" and others as "South Mail Road."). This marks a good spot to turn around.

Buckley Creek Barrens Trail
Buckley Creek Barrens State Natural Area

Day hikers can truly get back to nature with a walk through a pine barrens near the northern reach of the St. Croix National Scenic Riverway.

The Buckley Creek Barrens Trail is an undesignated out-and-back footpath that runs 1.2-miles round trip across the Buckley Creek Barrens State Natural Area west of Gordon. Late summer and early autumn mark the best time to hike, as spring will be wet and buggy.

To reach the trail, from U.S. Hwy. 53 in Gordon, head west on County Road Y. At about 4.4 miles, turn left/south onto South Lost Lake Road. After 4.3 miles, turn west onto Sunset

Drive then in about a mile right/north onto Carp's Creek Road. The road runs north/south through the state natural area. In about 1.5 miles, you'll see a footpath on both sides of the road. Park on the shoulder here so other vehicles can pass.

Returning ecosystem

Go east on the trail, which heads through Buckley Creek Barrens' higher elevations. The St. Croix River is a few miles to the east curving north.

In this region of Wisconsin, a number of wetlands and small lakes dot the landscape, surrounded by pine barrens – areas of sandy soil that support mainly pine and oak. The barrens once was the bottom of a glacial lake that existed at the end of the last ice age, some 10,000 years ago.

The trail is a biologist's dream, especially for those studying the rare pine barrens ecosystem. After years of preventing wildfires – which flora in a barrens depends upon to maintain their life cycle – one broke out in 1997. A barrens much like that which existed before white settlers came to the area more than a century before has returned, providing a living lab.

Beyond jack pine and hill's oak, among the trees that you can spot on the trail are black and pin cherry. The wetlands host a number of grasses.

Four rare butterflies

Because of this flora, butterflies and birds literally flock to the pine barrens. Among four rare Wisconsin butterfly species you might spot here are the cobweb skipper, the dusted skipper, Henry's elfin, and the Gorgone checkerspot. For birds, a number of thrashers, warblers and sparrows call the natural area home, and you might even spot an osprey or bald eagle overhead.

After 0.6 miles, the trail reaches a wetland's southeast tip. This marks a good spot to turn back.

State natural areas in Wisconsin typically don't have public facilities, and Buckley Creek Barrens is no exception. If you truly want to get into the wilds, this is a great hike. Be sure to use insect repellent and wear pants and long sleeves when walking the trail.

On the drive back to Gordon along County Road Y, you'll pass the Saint Croix Flowage. This man-made lake often is mistaken for the St. Croix River's headwaters; it's also not part of the national riverway.

Other Douglas County Trails

• **Brule Bog Boardwalk trail** – A boardwalk wends its way north of Lake St. Croix through the Brule Bog across a continental divide in which rivers on one side flow into Lake Superior while rivers on the other side flow into the mighty Mississippi. The trail is 4.6 miles round trip and fairly flat.

• **Brule River State Forest Annex Loop A** – North of Minong along County Road G lies a small area of planted forests along the Eau Claire River with multiple jeep trails running through it. From the end of the county road, hike west until the road curves north; take each of the three spur trails to the river for a 1.7-mile walk.

• **Brule-St. Croix Portage Trail** – People have used this trail for hundreds of years, most notably beginning in 1680 when French explorer Daniel Greysolon Sieur duLhut first noted the route linking the Brule and St. Croix rivers. The route is an easy 4.4-mile out-and-back trail with minimal elevation gain.

• **North Country National Scenic Trail, Douglas County Forest segment** – South of Solon Springs, the seven-state North Country Trail crosses the Douglas County Forest for roughly three miles. Along the way, it passes several idyllic ponds.

• **North Country National Scenic Trail, Solon Springs segment** – Before reaching the county forest, the trail cuts through the village. A pleasant 2-mile route runs south of town to the county forest from South Holly Lucius Road/U.S. Hwy. 53 to Bird Sanctuary Road at the forest's edge.

• **Wild Rivers State Trail, Solon Springs segment** – The rail line turned hiking path also runs through Solon Springs on its way between Gordon and Superior. To avoid highway noise, take the roughly 4-mile route heading north from the municipal airport to County Road L.

• For more Douglas County hikes, see this title's sister book, **Day Hiking Trails of Douglas County**.

Bayfield County

From Trego, U.S. Hwy. 63 heads through northwest Sawyer County into southern Bayfield County. Most notable in southern Bayfield County is the scenic village of Cable, a gateway to the Chequamegon State Forest.

Birkie Trail
Birkebeiner Trail system

Though known primarily for the annual ski race held on it, Wisconsin's massive Birkebeiner Trail system also makes a great hiking route in summer.

With more than 66 miles of trails, all maintained by the nonprofit American Birkebeiner Ski Foundation, "The Birkie Trail," as its fans affectionately call it, offers multiple trailheads, loops and variations between Cable and Hayward. One segment that's easy to locate and hike is the Birkie's opening section, a 2.6-mile round trip when treated as an out-and-back trail.

Classic Northern hardwoods

To reach the trailhead, in Cable from County Road M go south onto Randysek Road. After crossing the Namekagon River, turn left/east onto McNaught Road. Drive about 1.7 miles then park to the side of one of the mowed paths on the road's left/north side.

After walking through the treeline, the Cable Union Airport comes into the view. The trail heads west from the airport.

Built for bicycling and cross-country skiing races, Birkie Ridge is wide and void of roots and stones.

The entire opening segment of the trail runs through a classic Northern hardwoods forest of sugar maple, basswood, beech, white ash, and yellow birch, making for a colorful autumn walk. Hemlock and fir also appear in the mix.

The opening segment also sits inside the St. Croix National Scenic Riverway. The Namekagon River, protected by the National Park Service unit, flows north of the trail on its way to Hayward.

Forty-plus years in the making

The entire Birkie trail system is a 40-plus year project in the making. The first cross-country ski race was held on it in 1973; today, it's the largest race of its kind in North America, attracting about 10,000 participants and 15,000 spectators.

Northwoods promoter Tony Wise is largely credited with starting the race and helping to popularize modern-day cross-country skiing. In 1972, he built cross-country trails at his Telemark Ski Area near Cable then a year later started the Birkie race.

The Birkie trail system gets its name from Norway's Birkebeinerrennet cross-country event, which commemorates when skiers in 1206 AD smuggled the king's illegitimate son to safety during a civil war. The skiers were soldiers in the Birkebiener party.

Upon reaching the power line, the trail veers southeast and crosses McNaught Road. The power line marks a good point to turn back.

Be aware that mountain bikers and joggers also use the Birkie. There's plenty of space for both, but on race days the trail system will be closed to hikers; check *birkie.com/trail* to see when events are planned.

Forest Lodge Nature Trail
Chequamegon National Forest

Among the best hikes to learn about the Wisconsin North-woods is the Forest Lodge Nature Trail, east of Cable. Located in the Chequamegon National Forest, the 1.5-mile loop is maintained in cooperation with the Cable Natural History Museum.

Any dry summer day is excellent for hiking the trail, and fall colors are spectacular with trees usually remaining golden until the third week in October.

To reach the trail, take County Road M for about 8.6 miles east of Cable. Turn left/north on Garmish Road. The trailhead is a mile later on the road's right/south side.

From the parking lot, head straight south into an old field. If you turn left, you'll end up on the neighboring Conservancy Trail.

Spruce, bog, white pine

While fairly flat, the trail does narrow from four- to two-feet wide upon reaching the woods. The forested section of the trail sports some rough tread as well.

The trail rambles through a number of ecosystems, offering a mini-walk through the region's natural history.

Among the ecosystems is a lowland bog, surrounded by spruce and slender-stemmed cotton grass. Here you'll also find the carnivorous bog-dwelling pitcher plant.

Another ecosystem – now rare for northern Wisconsin – is of old-growth white pines. During the 1880s when pioneers settled the area, the white pine dominated; after being logged off, hardwoods replaced them.

A good portion of the trail is a newer upland hardwood forest. Chipmunks are abundant there.

Giant boulders

One element of the landscape hasn't changed, though: glacial erratics. These are boulders and rocks brought here during the last ice age that are different in color and composition than those "native" to the area.

Hikers also will walk through a grove of hemlocks, which looks like a scene out of a fairy tale, and an experimental prairie.

An excellent way to identify and learn more about these sights is the interpretive booklet available at the Cable Natural History Museum, located in Cable at 13470 County Road M (check ahead for hours).

If time and energy permits, consider adding the two-mile Conservancy Trail to your hike. That trail is more varied in terrain with some hill climbing.

Other Bayfield Country Trails

• **Namekagon Trail East Loop** – Located northeast of Cable in the Chequamegon National Forest, the 1-mile East Loop of this three-loop trail can be hiked in summer. You're very likely to hear and possibly even spot Northwoods wildlife along the walk.

• **North End Trail** – South of town, this ski trail in winter is often day hiked the other seasons. Consisting of several crisscrossing routes, combine the Ridge and Bear Paw loops for a 1.6-mile walk.

• **Rock Lake Trail** – Narrow loops of varying lengths run through the Chequamegon around Rock, Frels and Hildebrand lakes. Hiking is best on the segments running from Forest Road 207 to any of these waterbodies.

• For more Bayfield County hikes, see this title's sister book, **Day Hiking Trails of Bayfield County**.

Sawyer County

The St. Croix National Scenic Riverway heads from Washburn County east into Sawyer County. The riverway and area centered on the outdoors-minded community of Hayward provides a number of hiking opportunities.

Namekagon-Laccourt Oreilles Portage Trail
St. Croix National Scenic Riverway

Though the Namekagon-Laccourt Oreilles Portage Trail memorializes a famous 18th century route where fur traders and explorers carried their canoes between rivers, hikers will head through a landscape much changed from that day. In fact, those fur traders and explorers probably wouldn't recognize the wild area.

Located near Hayward in the St. Croix National Scenic Riverway, the modern trail is very close to the original portage route. A fur trader even operated a winter post during 1784 near the trail.

That portage route sprung up because travelers hoping to avoid problems with Sioux Indians near the St. Croix and Mississippi rivers junction decided to instead reach the continent's greatest waterway downstream from the Sioux by making a series of portages from the Namekagon to the Chippewa River, which joins the Mississippi at Lake Pepin.

To reach the portage trail, from Hayward go south on Wis. Hwy. 27. A historic marker erected in 1955 commemorates the portage. Turn left/west onto Rainbow Road then right/north onto Rolf Road. Upon entering the scenic riverway, take the first left/west. A parking lot will be on the right, and the trailhead begins there.

Significantly different

An easy, 0.8-mile loop, hikers will head through a second

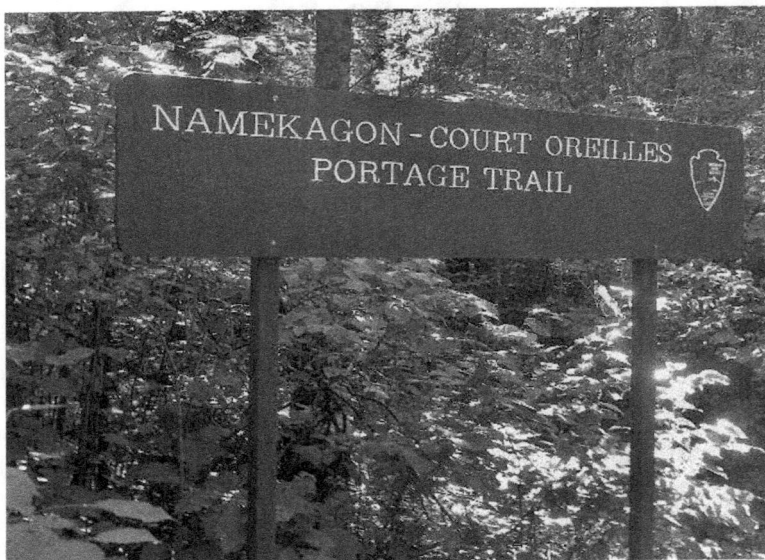

Note that the name on the trailhead sign for the Namekagon-Laccourt Oreilles Portage Trail doesn't match what's on trail maps or brochures.

growth forest of mixed hardwoods and pines.

Those using the portage trail in the 1700s found quite different flora growing there. At the time, this flat sandy area largely consisted of red and jack pines with white pines on the surrounding higher grounds. Most of that was logged off during the late 1800s, however, and the result is an area now dominated by maples, oaks, birch, red pine and spruce.

Logging and later small dams collaborated to change life in the Namekagon by leaving the shoreline open to sunlight. The result was an increase in the water temperature, which decimated some fish populations common during fur trading times.

Spur to riverfront

At the loop's westernmost edge, hikers can take a short

spur trail to the Namekagon, and it's well worth the walk for the blue river is scenic.

One thing the 101-mile long tributary to the St. Croix River does retain is its Ojibwa name, which means "at the place abundant with sturgeons."

Today, bass, blacknose dace, brook trout, brown trout, cheek chub, Johnny Darter, mudminnow, northern pike, sculpin and sucker primarily live in the river. Rainbow Creek, which runs south of trail and feeds the Namekagon, remains a rainbow trout fishery, however.

Along the trail, hikers also can cross wetlands over a boardwalk. Watch and listen for bull frogs, turtles and waterfowl that are common in the area.

Totagatic River State Wildlife Area jeep trail
Totagatic River State Wildlife Area

Day hikers can ramble alongside one of Wisconsin's few remaining wilderness streams on a jeep trail in the Totagatic River State Wildlife Area.

Though not a designated trail, the old logging road runs about a mile (2-miles round trip) through a forested area along the Totagatic Flowage's northwest side. The flowage marks a wide swath of the meandering Totagatic River, which in 2009 became Wisconsin's fifth stream to receive Wild River status.

To reach the trailhead, from Hayward take Wis. Hwy. 77 north/west. Turn left/north onto Wis. Hwy. 27. Park off the road on the west side of Hwy. 27 across from Dam Road. The jeep trail heads northwest from the parking area.

Most of the trail is under the cover of northern hard-woods, which makes for a scenic walk during autumn.

The Totagatic runs 70 miles through five counties. Its headwaters are in southern Bayfield County. Popular among canoeists, the cold and clear river flows into Totagatic Lake then to Nelson Lake and into the flowage. Hwy. 27 and the dam split Nelson Lake from the flowage.

Expect to spot a number of waterfowl along the hike. The bird-friendly flowage was constructed in the 1950s, and the 272-acre Totagatic River Wildlife Area has long been designated a state waterfowl restoration area. A mix of habitats – from hardwood forests and open water to swamps and upland grasslands – make up the wildlife area.

If you ask locals about the river or read printed materials on it, you're likely to run into some confusing appellations. Spellings and pronunciations of the river are about as murky as its name suggests – "Totagatic" is derived from the Ojibwa word "Totogan," which translates as "boggy river." Maps, plat books, tour guides variously spell the river's name as "Totagatic" and "Totogatic." Local pronunciations range from "Tuh-TO-ga-tec" and "To-TA-ga-tec" to "To-to-GAT-ic" and "To-BA-tec."

From the flowage, the river heads roughly west. Northwest of Minong, it turns south and eventually flows into the Namekagon River.

Back in the wildlife area, the trail peters out at the edge of the flowage, a grasslands that the river runs through the center of. As an old logging road, expect parts of the trail to be overgrown, so don jeans and insect repellent for the hike.

Other Sawyer Country Trails

• **Blue and Orange trails** – Among the Northwoods' newest hiking trails can be found at the Town of Hayward Recreational Forest. Combining the rec forest's Blue and Orange trails into a 1.6-mile walk takes you through a woods then past a wetland and a scenic lake where wildlife is abundant.

• **Tuscobia State Trail** – East of Couderay, the trail runs

alongside the Couderay River. Access the trail where it crosses Valesh Road south of Wis. Hwy. 70.

• **West Torch Trail** – Northeast of town, a trio of stacked
loops form the West Torch Trail in the Chequamegon National Forest. From the parking lot, take the first (and shortest) of
the loops for a roughly 2-mile hike through a wooded area.

• For more Sawyer County hikes, see this title's sister
book, **Day Hiking Trails of Sawyer County**.

Rusk County

Birchwood marks a good springboard for exploring northern Rusk County, which includes the scenic Blue Hills, an ancient geological formation popular among hikers, campers and fishermen.

Blue Hills West Trail

Across northwest Barron County and northwest Rusk County, a hazy blue stretch of hills appearing vaguely like distant mountains offers a scenic backdrop. The site is the ancient Blue Hills, a range that runs for about 20 miles, primarily in Rusk County.

Several miles of footpaths meander through the Blue Hills. They generally are associated with one of three major trail groups:

• **Ice Age National Scenic Trail** – Trailheads to various segments are located on Old 14/Bass Lake Road, Bolgers Road and Bucks Lake Road.

• **Blue Hills East Trail** – Fourteen stacked loops over a variety of terrain are used by cross-country skiers in winter but can be day hiked other seasons on a system maintained by the Blue Hills Trail Association.

• **Blue Hills West Trail** – This sister set of cross country ski trails includes two stacked loops and a lollipop trail.

The Blue Hills West Trail's first stacked loop at 2.3 miles total is particularly good for day hiking.

To reach it, from Spooner, take U.S. Hwy. 53 south then U.S. Hwy. 8 east to Weyerhaeuser. In the village, turn left/north on Second Street. Take the road out of town for about seven miles. At the Y intersection, turn right/east. After passing Christie Mountain, turn left/north onto Fire Lane Road. Next, go left/west onto Excelsior Road (unmarked); if you pass the turnoff for the East Side Trailhead and parking

The naturally rocky surface of the Blue Hills West Trail

lot, you've gone too far.

Rocky Wisconsin high

The West Side trailhead is on the parking lot's north side; this is Junction A. All intersections are signed with "you-are-here" maps, and junctions are labeled with an alphabet letter.

As the trail heads northwest, you're at about 1375 feet elevation, which may not be much compared to the Rockies or the Appalachians, but for Wisconsin there are few spots that are higher. In the Midwest, these are the equivalent of mountains.

The Blue Hills formed more than 1.7 billion years ago when sediment settled across a flat plain submerged in shallow water. With each new layer of sediment, the sands below cemented into a hard, glittery rock known as red quartzite. The quartzite now runs 600 feet thick and is highly resistant to erosion.

After about 0.45 miles of walking, you'll reach Junction B. Go left/west. The terrain gradually will start climbing in elevation.

At the base of these hills, you'll notice sloping piles of fallen rocks, called felsenmeer. Though smooth sided, their edges are very sharp, so be careful if picking them up.

In a little less than two-thirds of a mile, the trail comes to Junction C. Go right/north.

In addition to being careful with the sharp rocks, avoid stepping on or picking any plants growing in the felsenmeer. Several endangered species live in this unique environment.

Colorful fall foliage

In about a fifth of a mile, you'll reach Junction I. Go right/west for 0.58 miles. Johns Creek flows to the trail's left, but in short order the stream and footpath angle away from one another, and you descend toward the trailhead.

The Blue Hills primarily sits in a mixed deciduous forest, but you also can find red and white pines, balsam, and hemlock. Because of this, late September and early October mark a good time to hike the trails for the fall foliage. Be aware that hunting occurs during some parts of autumn.

At Junction J, go right/south. This returns you to Junction

B, where you go left back to the parking lot.

For amenities, pit toilets are at the trailhead. As the trails are maintained by a private, nonprofit organization, please give a donation if you can to support their upkeep.

Other Rusk Country Trails

• **Devils Creek State Wildlife Management Area trails** – Bring a fishing pole and follow a Class I trout stream on this unmarked trail. From Weyerhaeuser, take County Road F north for a little more than six miles; at the Y intersection with County Road O, turn right. Where the road crosses Devils Creek, park off the shoulder and head south along the creek.

Barron County

If taking U.S. Hwy. 53 into Washburn County, you'll be tempted to stop at the number of great recreational areas along a chain of lakes from Chetek to Rice Lake. U.S. Hwy 63 also offers some major attractions, most notably in the Cumberland region.

Wild Rivers State Trail, Rice Lake segment

A walk through pleasant woodlands and scenic farmland await users of the Wild Rivers State Trail near Rice Lake. The trail runs for around 100 miles across three counties on an old Omaha and Soo Line Railroads rail line connecting the city to Superior.

A good place to experience the trail is at its southern end. Park north of the Rice Lake city limits at the Tuscobia State Trail junction on County Road SS, near its intersection with U.S. Hwy. 53. Head south for about four miles into Rice Lake at West Knapp Street. Arrange to have someone bring you back to where you parked, or turn around at any time.

The parking lot sits east of County Road SS, and you'll need to take the Tuscobia Trail west across the highway to reach the Wild Rivers Trail. Turn left or south onto the Wild Rivers Trail, which parallels County Road SS into Rice Lake. Turn right, and the trail heads to Haugen, Spooner, Trego, Minong, Gordon, Solon Springs and ends in Superior.

In addition to plenty of parking and its proximity to a major town for an enjoyable meal or shopping afterward, the part of the trail heading south is in excellent shape with compacted gravel making up the surface.

The first half mile or so heads through a typical deciduous forest that Wisconsin is famous for. In autumn, the trail's varied trees alight in an array of crimson, amber and burnt orange leaves. Upon crossing County Road BB, however, the

Wild Rivers State Trail trailhead near Rice Lake

woods gives way to pretty farm fields that look best when green in August.

A little more than two miles later, you can glimpse through the deepening treeline a tributary that ultimately flows into nearby Stump Lake. As the region becomes more wooded, you'll actually cross the serpentine waterway over a quaint bridge.

Expect to spot white-tailed deer, rabbits, squirrels and chipmunks – and if lucky, fox – along the way. Songbirds are plentiful, and hawks soar overhead.

On weekends, anticipate a variety of other users. Mountain bikers, horseback riders and ATVers also frequent the trail. In winter, snowmobilers, cross country skiers and snowshoers all use the route.

The trail grows increasingly urban as reaching 22-1/2 Street with a good end spot at Knapp Street, where you can park your vehicle. Pit toilets are available at the trailhead.

Ice Age National Scenic Trail, Waterman Lake segment

Waterman Lake Area County Forest

Day hikers will have several opportunities to spot the impressive white-tailed deer on a segment of the Ice Age National Scenic Trail in northwest Barron County.

The 2.6-miles round trip segment of the Ice Age Trail runs through Waterman Lake Area County Forest. The Ice Age Trail runs 1200 miles across the state, mostly marking the farthest advance of the last glacier to touch these parts some 11,000 years ago.

To reach the trailhead, from Cumberland, take U.S. Hwy 63 north. Turn left/west onto 24-1/2 Avenue. The road becomes 4th Street when it begins running along Beaver Dam Lake and gradually curves north. When 4th Street splits, the main road turns west and becomes County Road H/3-1/2 Street, passing several farms, then upon veering north turns to 3rd Street. After the 29-1/2 Street intersection, look for the gravel parking lot on the road's left/west side. Park there.

Take the access trail from the lot's northwest corner for about 0.05 miles to the Ice Age Trail. Go left/southwest onto the Ice Age Trail. The trail generally heads south through a mixed hardwoods forest. This habitat is perfect for white-tailed deer, which often grazes on agricultural fields at the edge of woodlands.

In about 0.6 miles, you'll reach a junction to a side trail; continue right/west. In about 0.1 miles, you'll come to the junction for where the side trail reconnects with the main trail.

Wisconsin's official wildlife animal, white-tailed deer are quite common across the state. They can grow up to three-feet high at the shoulder and weigh up to 200 pounds.

As heading west, wetlands areas can be found off both

Waterman Lake Area County Forest

sides of the trail. At 0.8 miles from trailhead, you'll junction a trail heading north; continue left/west on the main trail, though.

Fawns usually are born in May and June, so a great time to hike this trail is late summer when mothers bring out their young. Newborns typically remain low in the grass, and their

reddish brown coats with white spots makes for perfect cam-
ouflage.

About 1.1 miles in, the trail turns northwest coming along
the shoreline of Lake 4-8. This is a good location to spy
whitetail taking a drink.

Should you spot a deer, unless it is in the distance or
freezes, don't expect to see it for long. Despite long skinny
legs, they can run up to 40 miles per hour, jump nine feet
high (allowing them to clear almost any fence), and can swim
about 13 miles per hour. When broad jumping, they can leap
up to 30 feet in a single bound.

At 1.25 miles from the trailhead, the Ice Age Trail veers
away from lake; upon reaching a junction with a trail heading
north, turn back. The trail does continue west through the
county forest, but the landscape gets significantly swampier
for the next mile or so.

Other Barron Country Trails

Rice Lake area
• **Cedar Lake Area County Forest trails** – As with all Barron County Forests, several unnamed trails crisscross the
wooded area. Try the northern-most one, off of Valley Road,
which heads west for 2.5 miles through a nice mix of hardwoods; it ends at a gate just shy of Red Cedar Lake.
• **Cedar Lake Sections 5 & 6 County Forest** – Off of
North Townline Road just east of 24th Street, a trail runs
roughly north-south for about 1.5 miles before coming to a T-
intersection. You'll walk through a thick hardwood forest.
• **Cedar Side Walking Trail** – If you need to make a trip
into town, consider this beautiful trail that runs alongside the
Red Cedar River. Plenty wide and some of it paved, you can
take different-length segments based on your abilities.
• **Ice Age National Scenic Trail, Cedar Lake Area
County Forest segment** – Directly south of Birchwood, the

Ice Age Trail cuts roughly north-south through the Cedar Lake Area County Forest. Take the forest's easternmost jeep trail off Lemler Lane and pick up the Ice Age Trail for a 3.5-mile walk one way to Pigeon Creek.

• **Mikana Area County Forest** – On Swamp Road upon coming to Mirror Lake, take the gated trail going north. You'll skirt the shorelines of the lake and then Lake 20-10. For about a 1-mile round trip, turnaround at the gate where the trail splits.

• **Moon Lake Biking and Walking Trail** – Located at the site of a former municipal airport, this 1.5-mile round trip trail heads to and along scenic Moon Lake. The trail is wide and paved.

• **Tuscobia State Trail** – Built on old railroad tracks, the Tuscobia State Trail shares a stretch with the Ice Age Trail as it heads northeast. The trail runs about three miles to the 22nd Street intersection.

Cumberland area

• **Bear Lake Area County Forest trails** – A large number of trails crisscross this Barron County forest. Entering from the north side on Narrow Gauge Road, take the first gated trail on the left for a half-mile round trip to Lake 6.

• **Black Duck Lake Trail** – On County Road H south of 29th Avenue, take the gated jeep trail at Waterman Lake Area County Forest heading west. You'll walk past Lake 9-8A (It's more of a pond, really.) and end at scenic Black Duck Lake for a 2-mile round trip. Wear pants as the frog-laden grass can be high in summer.

• **Kirby Lake Area County Forest trails** – On Fifth Street just before the road curves toward Kirby Lake, turn east onto a gated jeep trail. The path heads to Tamarack Lake; at the T-intersection, turn back for a 1.4-mile round trip.

• **Maple Plain Area County Forest trails** – From 29-1/2

Avenue, take the gated jeep trail heading south. The trail crosses an unnamed creek flowing into Upper Waterman Lake. At the T-intersection, turn back for a half-mile round trip.

• For more Barron County hikes, see this title's sister book, **Day Hiking Trails of Barron County**.

Burnett County

Two major routes run from Washburn County through forest-laden lands into Burnett County. From Spooner, take Wis. Hwy. 70 west to Siren; from Minong, head west on Wis. Hwy. 77 to Danbury and the St. Croix River.

Big Bear Lake Nature Trails
Burnett County Forest

The Big Bear Lake Nature Trails offer three great day hiking opportunities for those in the lake country of Burnett County.

All three trails are accessible from the same trailhead. The Grouse Walk Trail is the shortest at a half-mile.

To reach the trails, from Minong take Wis. Hwy. 77 west. Turn left/south onto Bear Lake Road; in about 1.5 miles, turn left/east into a sand parking lot. If you've reached the Lake 26 Road intersection, you've missed the lot.

From the trailhead at the parking lot, go straight (the middle route). Going left takes you to the Big Bear Springs Trail for a 0.75-mile loop, which is fairly similar to the Grouse Walk Trail.

You're now heading clockwise on Grouse Walk Trail through a largely open grassland and shrubland with scattered pines, so you'll definitely need hat and sunscreen for the hike.

The nature trails are located in the rare Northwest Sands ecological landscape, which angles across this corner of Wisconsin from the St. Croix River to just short of the Lake Superior.

Farm crops can't readily grow here because all that separates the surface from underlying bedrock is glacial drift – sand, gravel and silt left during the last ice age.

About midway through the Grouse Walk loop, an inter-

The Grouse Walk of the Big Bea Lake Nature Trails

secting trail takes you east to the Big Bear Meadows Trail. The trail is more wooded and runs for 0.875 miles.

After curving southwest, the Grouse Walk loop skirts the shoreline of a small pond that often is just a shallow depression during dry years. The loamy nature of the soil typically means that moisture drains fast through it.

Despite that, a number of kettle lakes from melted chunks of an ice age glacier exist across the region. Among them is nearby Big Bear Lake; though these nature trails are named for it, that lake actually is a good half-mile to the northeast.

Circling to Grouse Walk loop's south side, you'll head through a small grove. Pine, aspen, birch and oak dominate the few stands of trees in the Northwest Sands. Upon existing the stand, you'll have returned to the parking lot.

Namekagon Delta Trail
St. Croix National Scenic Riverway

Families can day hike to a scenic delta at the confluence of the St. Croix and Namekagon rivers.

A number of unnamed and non-maintained trails run near the delta in the St. Croix National Scenic Riverway. For convenience's sake, we've named this 2.7-mile out-and-back trail the Namekagon Delta Trail after its primary geographic feature.

Some of the area that the trail crosses, including the confluence itself, actually is part of the Big Island State Natural Area, but the boundaries with the scenic riverway are indistinguishable.

Like a wishbone, the national scenic riverway splits in Burnett County. One fork – the St. Croix River – continues northward to its headwaters while the other fork – the Namekagon River – heads eastward.

To reach the trailhead, from Minong take Wis. Hwy. 77 west. Just north of Danbury, take Wis. Hwy. 35 north. Turn right/east onto the paved road named Springbrook Trail (If you've crossed the St. Croix River, you've just missed the turn.). Next, turn left/north onto Namekagon Point Road. The road stops at a vista of the Namekagon and St. Croix's confluence, which sits about 94 feet below. Park off to the side of the road.

Take the jeep trail that heads to the left/northwest. It quickly descends about 90 feet to the river valley, heading through a woods to the confluence for a half-mile.

The St. Croix's largest tributary, the Namekagon meanders for 101 miles, crossing four Wisconsin counties. It's a major recreational area, with a number of boat landings and campsites, especially in Washburn and Sawyer counties.

The Namekagon Delta includes a sandbar that doesn't quite cut the St. Croix's width in half, but it does narrow the flow by diminishing the latter's depth. Only a hundred feet or so south of the delta, the St. Croix widens to the same distance as it was north of the confluence.

Heading back up the cliffside to the vista site, take the fairly flat primitive trail running southwest along the bluff line. Its trailhead is along Namekagon Point Road just south of the vista.

The bluff line stretch of the trail runs for 0.85 miles one way, offering views of the confluence and then the St. Croix River in the tree breaks. The large island in the St. Croix's center is Big Island. Where the primitive trail reaches a jeep trail (listed on some maps as "Snowmobile Trail") marks a good turnaround point.

During spring into late summer, mosquito repellant is a necessity at the confluence.

Other Burnett Country Trails

• **Gandy Dancer Trail (Siren segment)** – For a pleasant return to small town America, day hike this trail, which runs north-south through the village of Siren. Start downtown and head north to the airport for a four-mile round trip hike. To reach the trail, park downtown in the northwest quadrant of Wis. Hwys. 35 and 70 intersection. The trail parallels Hwy. 35 so can be accessed by simply taking any street west.

• **Gandy Dancer Trail (Webster segment)** – A scenic

segment of the Gandy Dancer State Trail runs for two miles north of Webster from the Yellow River to Yellow Lake at Lone Pine Road. As with most rail lines turned hiking trails, the former railroad corridor is flat. And despite that this section in Burnett County is close to built-up areas, it's fairly tranquil.

• **Loon Creek Trail** – A plethora of snowmobile trails crisscross Burnett County, and during summer many of them can be day hiked. One good hub for these trails is the Burnett County Forest's Loon Creek Trailhead. From it, the Loon Creek Trail (so christened here for convenience's sake) runs about 4-miles round trip over snowmobile/ATV routes. To reach the trailhead, from Minong go east on Hwy. 77. Turn south/left onto Bear Lake Road. At Lake 26 Road, go right/ west, then at the next intersection, left/south onto Loon Creek Trail. A large parking lot is on the road's left/east side just before Deerpath Road.

• **Timberland Hills Ski Trails** – As with snowmobile trails, sometimes cross country ski trails also can be used a hiking trails in summer. One such system is in the Burnett County Forest. To reach it, from south of Shell Lake on U.S. Hwy. 63, go right/west on to County Road J; turn left/south onto County Road H then straight/east onto Boyd Road to the trailhead.

• For more Burnett County hikes, see this title's sister books, **Day Hiking Burnett County, Wisconsin** and **Day Hiking Crex Meadows Wildlife Area.**

Best Trails Lists

W hich trails are the best for watching birds? To enjoy fall colors? Walking the family dog? Here are some lists of the best Washburn County trails for those and many other specific interests.

Autumn leaves
• Trego Lake Trail
• Gordon Flowage Campground Trail (Douglas County)
• Wild Rivers Trail, Rice Lake segment (Barron County)

Birdwatching
• Bear Trail
• Beaver Brook East Trail
• Wild Rivers Trail, Trego segment

Campgrounds
• Gordon Flowage Campground Trail (Douglas County)

Dog-friendly
• Beaver Brook East Trail
• Trego Lake Trail
• Trego Nature Trail

Geology
• Forest Lodge Nature Trail (Bayfield County)
• Blue Hills West Trail (Rusk County)

History/Archeology
• Wild Rivers Trail, Spooner segment

Must-do's
• Bear Trail
• Trego Lake Trail
• Trego Nature Trail

Plant communities
• Bear Trail
• Blue Hills West Trail (Rusk County)
• Buckley Creek Barrens Trail (Douglas County)

Vistas
• Namekagon Delta Trail (Burnett County)

Wildflowers
• Bear Trail

Wildlife
• Ice Age National Scenic Trail
• Trego Nature Trail
• Namekagon Trail East Loop (Bayfield County)

Bonus Section:
Day Hiking Primer

Y ou'll get more out of a day hike if you research it and plan ahead. It's not enough to just pull over to the side of the road and hit a trail that you've never been on and have no idea where it goes. In fact, doing so invites disaster.

Instead, you should preselect a trail (This book's trail descriptions can help you do that). You'll also want to ensure that you have the proper clothing, equipment, navigational tools, first-aid kit, food and water. Knowing the rules of the trail and potential dangers along the way also are helpful. In this special section, we'll look at each of these topics to ensure you're fully prepared.

Selecting a Trail

For your first few hikes, stick to short, well-known trails where you're likely to encounter others. Once you get a feel for hiking, your abilities, and your interests, expand to longer and more remote trails.

Always check to see what the weather will be like on the trail you plan to hike. While an adult might be able to withstand wind and a sprinkle here or there, for kids it can be pure misery. Dry, pleasantly warm days with limited wind always are best when hiking with children.

Don't choose a trail that is any longer than the least fit person in your group can hike. Adults in good shape can go 8-12 miles a day; for kids, it's much less. There's no magical number.

When planning the hike, try to find a trail with a mid-point payoff – that is something you and definitely any children will find exciting about half-way through the hike. This will help keep up everyone's energy and enthusiasm during the journey.

If you have children in your hiking party, consider a couple of additional points when selecting a trail.

Until children enter their late teens, they need to stick to trails rather than going off-trail hiking, which is known as bushwhacking. Children too easily can get lost when off trail. They also can easily get scratched and cut up or stumble across poisonous plants and dangerous animals.

Generally, kids will prefer a circular route to one that requires hiking back the way you came. The return trip often feels anti-climatic, but you can overcome that by mentioning features that all of you might want to take a closer look at.

Once you select a trail, it's time to plan for your day hike. Doing so will save you a lot of grief – and potentially prevent an emergency – later on. You are, after all, entering the wilds, a place where help may not be readily available.

When planning your hike, follow these steps:

• Print a road map showing how to reach the parking lot near the trailhead. Outline the route with a transparent yellow highlighter and write out the directions.

• Print a satellite photo of the parking area and the trailhead. Mark the trailhead on the photo.

• Print a topo map of the trail. Outline the trail with the yellow highlighter. Note interesting features you want to see along the trail and the destination.

• If carrying GPS, program this information into your device.

• Make a timeline for your trip, listing: when you will leave home; when you will arrive at the trailhead; your turn back time; when you will return for home in your vehicle; and when you will arrive at your home.

• Estimate how much water and food you will need to bring based on the amount of time you plan to spend on the trail and in your vehicle. You'll need at least two pints of water per person for every hour on the trail.

• Fill out two copies of a hiker's safety form. Leave one in your vehicle.

• Share all of this information with a responsible person remaining in civilization, leaving a hiker's safety form with them. If they do not hear from you within an hour of when you plan to leave the trail in your vehicle, they should contact authorities to report you as possibly lost.

Clothing

Footwear

If your feet hurt, the hike is over, so getting the right footwear is worth the time. Making sure the footwear fits before hitting the trail also is worth it. With children, if you've gone a few weeks without hiking, that's plenty of time for feet to grow, and they may have just outgrown their hiking boots. Check out everyone's footwear a few days before heading out on the hike. If it doesn't fit, replace it.

For flat, smooth, dry trails, sneakers and cross-trainers are fine; but if you really want to head onto less traveled roads or tackle areas that aren't typically dry, you'll need hiking boots. Once you start doing any rocky or steep trails – and remember that a trail you consider moderately steep needs to be only half that angle for a child to consider it extremely steep – you'll want hiking boots, which offer rugged tread perfect for handling rough trails.

Socks

Socks serve two purposes: to wick sweat away from skin

and to provide cushioning. Cotton socks aren't very good for hiking, except in extremely dry environments, because they retain moisture that can lead to blisters. Wool socks or liner socks work best. You'll want to look for three-season socks, also known as trekking socks. While a little thicker than summer socks, their extra cushioning generally prevents blisters. Also, make sure kids don't put on holey socks; that's just inviting blisters.

Layering

On all but hot, dry days, when hiking you should wear multiple layers of clothing that provide various levels of protection against sweat, heat loss, wind and potentially rain. Layering works because the type of clothing you select for each stratum serves a different function, such as wicking moisture or shielding against wind. In addition, trapped air between each layer of clothing is warmed by your body heat. Layers also can be added or taken off as needed.

Generally, you need three layers. Closest to your skin is the wicking layer, which pulls perspiration away from the body and into the next layer, where it evaporates. Exertion from walking means you will sweat and generate heat, even if the weather is cold. The second layer provides insulation, which helps keep you warm. The last layer is a water-resistant shell that protects you from rain, wind, snow and sleet.

As the seasons and weather change, so does the type of clothing you select for each layer. The first layer ought to be a loose-fitting T-shirt in summer, but in winter and on other cold days you might opt for a long-sleeved moisture-wicking synthetic material, like polypropylene. During winter, the next layer probably also should cover the neck, which often is exposed to the elements. A turtleneck works fine, but preferably not one made of cotton. The third layer in winter, depending on the temperature, could be a wool sweater, a half-zippered long sleeved fleece jacket, or a fleece vest.

You might even add a fourth layer of a hooded parka with pockets, made of material that can block wind and resist water. Gloves or mittens as well as a hat also are necessary on cold days.

Headgear

Half of all body heat is lost through the head, hence the hiker's adage, "If your hands are cold, wear a hat." In cool, wet weather, wearing a hat is at least good for avoiding hypothermia, a potentially deadly condition in which heat loss occurs faster than the body can generate it. Children are more susceptible to hypothermia than adults.

Especially during summer, a hat with a wide brim is useful in keeping the sun out of eyes. It's also nice should rain start falling.

For young children, get a hat with a chin strap. They like to play with their hats, which will fly off in a wind gust if not fastened some way to the child.

Sunglasses

Sunglasses are an absolute must if walking through open areas exposed to the sun and in winter when you can suffer from snow blindness. Look for 100% UV-protective shades, which provide the best screen.

Equipment

A couple of principles should guide your purchases. First, the longer and more complex the hike, the more equipment you'll need. Secondly, your general goal is to go light. Since you're on a day hike, the amount of gear you'll need is a fraction of what backpackers shown in magazines and cat-alogues usually carry. Still, the inclination of most day hikers is to not carry enough equipment. For the lightness is-sue, most gear today is made with titanium and siliconized nylon, ensuring it is sturdy yet fairly light. While the following list of what you need may look long, it won't weigh much.

Backpacks

Sometimes called daypacks (for day hikes or for kids), backpacks are essential to carry all of the essentials you need – snacks, first-aid kit, extra clothing.

For day hiking, you'll want to get yourself an internal frame, in which the frame giving the backpack its shape is inside the pack's fabric so it's not exposed to nature. Such frames usually are lightweight and comfortable.

External frames have the frame outside the pack, so they are exposed to the elements. They are excellent for long hikes into the backcountry when you must carry heavy loads, however.

As kids get older, and especially after they've been hiking for a couple of years, they'll want a "real" backpack. Unfortunately, most backpacks for kids are overbuilt and too heavy. Even light ones that safely can hold up to 50 pounds are inane for most children.

When buying a daypack for your child, look for sternum straps, which help keep the strap on the shoulders. This is vital for prepubescent children, as they do not have the broad shoulders that come with adolescence, meaning packs likely will slip off and onto their arms, making them uncomfortable and difficult to carry. Don't buy a backpack that a child will "grow into." Backpacks that don't fit well simply will lead to sore shoulder and back muscles and could result in poor posture.

Also, consider purchasing a daypack with a hydration system for kids. This will help ensure they drink a lot of water. More on this later when we get to canteens.

Before hitting the trail, always check your children's backpacks to make sure that they have not overloaded them. Kids think they need more than they really do. They also tend to overestimate their own ability to carry stuff. Sibling rivalries often lead to children packing more than they should in their rucksacks, too. Don't let them overpack "to teach them a lesson," though, as it can damage bones and turn the hike into a bad experience.

A good rule of thumb is no more than 25 percent capacity. Most upper elementary school kids can carry only about 10 pounds for any short distance. Subtract the weight of the backpack, and that means only 4-5 pounds in the backpack. Overweight children will need to carry a little less than this or they'll quickly be out of breath.

Child carriers

If your child is an infant or toddler, you'll have to carry him. Until infants can hold their heads up, which usually doesn't happen until about four to six months of age, a front pack (like a Snugli or Baby Bjorn) is best. It keeps the infant close for warmth and balances out your backpack. At the same time, though, you must watch for baby overheating in a front pack, so you'll need to remove the infant from your body at rest stops.

Once children reach about 20 pounds, they typically can hold their heads up and sit on their own. At that point, you'll want a baby carrier (sometimes called a child carrier or baby backpack), which can transfer the infant's weight to your hips when you walk. You'll not only be comfortable, but your child will love it, too.

Look for a baby carrier that is sturdy yet lightweight. Your child is going to get heavier as time passes, so about the only way you can counteract this is to reduce the weight of the items you use to carry things. The carrier also should have adjustment points, as you don't want your child to outgrow the carrier too soon. A padded waist belt and padded shoulder straps are necessary for your comfort. The carrier should provide some kind of head and neck support if you're hauling an infant. It also should offer back support for children of all ages, and leg holes should be wide enough so there's no chafing. You want to be able to load your infant without help, so it should be stable enough to stand that way when you take it off the child can sit in it for a moment while you get turned around. Stay away from baby carriers with only shoulder straps as you need the waist belt to help shift the child's weight to your hips for more comfortable walking.

Fanny packs

Also known as a belt bag, a fanny pack is virtually a must for anyone with a baby carrier as you can't otherwise lug a backpack. If your significant other is with you, he or she can carry the backpack, of course. Still, the fanny pack also is a good alternative to a backpack in hot weather, as it will reduce back sweat. If you have only one or two kids on a hike, or if they also are old enough to carry daypacks, your fanny pack need not be large. A mid-size pouch can carry at least 200 cubic inches of supplies, which is more than enough to accommodate all the materials you need. A good fanny pack also has a spot for hooking canteens to.

Canteens

Canteens or plastic bottles filled with water are vital for any hike, no matter how short the trail. You'll need to have enough of them to carry about two pints of water per person for every hour of hiking.

Trekking poles

Also known as walking poles or walking sticks, trekking

poles are necessary for maintaining stability on uneven or wet surfaces and to help reduce fatigue. The latter makes them useful on even surfaces. By transferring weight to the arms, a trekking pole can reduce stress on knees and lower back, allowing you to maintain a better posture and to go farther.

If an adult with a baby or toddler on your back, you'll primarily want a trekking pole to help you maintain your balance, even if on a flat surface, and to help absorb some of the impact of your step.

Graphite tips provide the best traction. A basket just above the tip is a good idea so the stick doesn't sink into mud or sand. Angled cork handles are ergonomic and help absorb sweat from your hands so they don't blister. A strap on the handle to wrap around your hand is useful so the stick doesn't slip out. Telescopic poles are a good idea as you can adjust them as needed based on the terrain you're hiking and as kids grow to accommodate their height.

The pole also needs to be sturdy enough to handle rugged terrain, as you don't want a pole that bends when you press it to the ground. Spring-loaded shock absorbers help when heading down a steep incline but aren't necessary. Indeed, for a short walk across flat terrain, the right length stick is about all you need.

Carabiners

Carabiners are metal loops, vaguely shaped like a D, with a sprung or screwed gate. You'll find that hooking a couple of them to your backpack or fanny pack useful in many ways. For example, if you need to dig through a fanny pack, you can hook the strap of your trekking pole to it. Your hat, camera straps, first-aid kit, and a number of other objects also can connect to them. Hook carabiners to your fanny pack or backpack upon purchasing them so you don't forget them when packing. Small carabiners with sprung gates are inexpensive, but they do have a limited life span of a couple of dozen hikes.

Navigational Tools
Paper maps

Paper maps may sound passé in this age of GPS, but you'll find the variety and breadth of view they offer to be useful. During the planning process, a paper map (even if viewing it online), will be far superior to a GPS device. On the hike, you'll also want a backup to GPS. Or like many casual hikers, you may not own GPS at all, which makes paper maps indispensable.

Standard road maps (which includes printed guides and handmade trail maps) show highways and locations of cities and parks. Maps included in guidebooks, printed guides handed out at parks, and those that are hand-drawn tend to be designed like road maps, and often carry the same positives and negatives.

Topographical maps give contour lines and other important details for crossing a landscape. You'll find them invaluable on a hike into the wilds. The contour lines' shape and their spacing on a topo map show the form and steepness of a hill or bluff, unlike the standard road map and most brochures and hand-drawn trail maps. You'll also know if you're in a woods, which is marked in green, or in a clearing, which is marked in white. If you get lost, figuring out where you are and how to get to where you need to be will be much easier with such information.

Satellite photos offer a view from above that is rendered exactly as it would look from an airplane. Thanks to Google and other online services, you can get fairly detailed pictures of the landscape. Such pictures are an excellent resource when researching a hiking trail. Unfortunately, those pictures don't label what a feature is or what it's called, as would a topo map. Unless there's a stream, determining if a feature is a valley bottom or a ridgeline also can be difficult. Like topo maps, satellite photos (most of which were taken by old Russian spy satellites), can be out of date a few years.

GPS

By using satellites, the global positioning system can find your spot on the Earth to within 10 feet. With a GPS device, you can preprogram the trailhead location and mark key turns and landmarks as well as the hike's end point. This mobile map is a powerful technological tool that almost certainly ensures you won't get lost – so long as you've correctly programmed the information. GPS also can calculate travel time and act as a compass, a barometer and altimeter, making such devices virtually obsolete on a hike.

In remote areas, however, reception is spotty at best for GPS, rendering your mobile map worthless. A GPS device also runs on batteries, and there's always a chance they will go dead. Or you may drop your device, breaking it in the process. Their screens are small, and sometimes you need a large paper map to get a good sense of the natural landmarks around you.

Compass

Like a paper map, a compass is indispensable even if you use GPS. Should your GPS no longer function, the compass then can be used to tell you which direction you're heading. A protractor compass is best for hiking. Beneath the compass needle is a transparent base with lines to help your orient yourself.

The compass often serves as a magnifying glass to help you make out map details. Most protractor compasses also come with a lanyard for easy carrying.

Food and Water

Water

As water is the heaviest item you'll probably carry, there is a temptation to not take as much as one should. Don't skimp on the amount of water you bring, though; after all, it's the one supply your body most needs. It's always better to end up having more water than you needed than returning to your vehicle dehydrated.

How much water should you take? Adults need at least a quart for every two hours hiking. Children need to drink about a quart every two hours of walking and more if the weather is hot or dry. To keep kids hydrated, have them drink at every rest stop.

Don't presume there will be water on the hiking trail. Most trails outside of urban areas lack such amenities. In addition, don't drink water from local streams, lakes, rivers or ponds. There's no way to tell if local water is safe or not. As soon as you have consumed half of your water supply, you should turn around for the vehicle.

Food

Among the many wonderful things about hiking is that snacking between meals isn't frowned upon. Unless going on an all-day hike in which you'll picnic along the way, you want to keep everyone in your hiking party fed, especially as hunger can lead to lethargic and discontented children. It'll also keep young kids from snacking on the local flora or dirt. Before hitting the trail, you'll want to repackage as much of the food as possible as products sold at grocery stores tend to come in bulky packages that take up space and add a little weight to your backpack. Place the food in re-sealable plastic bags.

Bring a variety of small snacks for rest stops. You don't want kids filling up on snacks, but you do need them to maintain their energy levels if they're walking or to ensure they don't turn fussy if riding in a child carrier. Go for complex carbohydrates and proteins for maintaining energy. Good options include dried fruits, jerky, nuts, peanut butter, prepared energy bars, candy bars with a high protein content (nuts, peanut butter), crackers, raisins and trail mix (called "gorp"). A number of trail mix recipes are available online; you and your children may want to try them out at home to see which ones you collectively like most.

Salty treats rehydrate better than sweet treats do. Chocolate and other sweets are fine if they're not all that's exclusively served, but remember they also tend to lead to thirst and to make sticky messes. Whichever snacks you choose, don't experiment with food on the trail. Bring what you know kids will like.

Give the first snack within a half-hour of leaving the trailhead or you risk children becoming tired and whiny from low energy levels. If kids start asking for them every few steps even after having something to eat at the last rest stop, consider timing snacks to reaching a seeable landmark, such as, "We'll get out the trail mix when we reach that bend up ahead."

Milk for infants

If you have an infant or unweaned toddler with you, milk is as necessary as water. Children who only drink breastfed milk but don't have their mother on the hike require that you have breast-pumped milk in an insulated beverage container (such as a Thermos) that can keep it cool to avoid spoiling. Know how much the child drinks and at what frequency so you can bring enough. You'll also need to carry the child's bottle and feeding nipples. Bring enough extra water in your canteen so you can wash out the bottle after each feeding. A handkerchief can be used to dry bottles between feedings.

Don't forget the baby's pacifier. Make sure it has a string and hook attached so it connects to the baby's outfit and isn't lost.

What not to bring

Avoid soda and other caffeinated beverages, alcohol, and energy pills. The caffeine will dehydrate children as well as you. Alcohol has no place on the trail; you need your full faculties when making decisions and driving home. Energy pills essentially are a stimulant and like alcohol can lead to bad calls. If you're tired, get some sleep and hit the trail another day.

First-aid Kit

After water, this is the most essential item you can carry.

A first-aid kit should include:

• Adhesive bandages of various types and sizes, especially butterfly bandages (for younger kids, make sure they're colorful kid bandages)

• Aloe vera

• Anesthetic (such as Benzocaine)

• Antacid (tablets)

• Antibacterial (aka antibiotic) ointment (such as Neosporin or Bacitracin)

• Anti-diarrheal tablets (for adults only, as giving this to a child is controversial)

• Anti-itch cream or calamine lotion

• Antiseptics (such as hydrogen peroxide, iodine or Betadine, Mercuroclear, rubbing alcohol)

• Baking soda

• Breakable (or instant) ice packs

• Cotton swabs

• Disposable syringe (w/o needle)

• Epipen (if children or adults have allergies)

- Fingernail clippers (your multi-purpose tool might have this, and if so you can dispense with it)
- Gauze bandage
- Gauze compress pads (2x2 individually wrapped pad)
- Hand sanitizer (use this in place of soap)
- Liquid antihistamine (not Benadryl tablets, however, as children should take liquid not pills; be aware that liquid antihistamines may cause drowsiness)
- Medical tape
- Moisturizer containing an anti-inflammatory
- Mole skin
- Pain reliever (aka aspirin; for children's pain relief, use liquid acetaminophen such Tylenol or liquid ibuprofen; never give aspirin to a child under 12)
- Poison ivy cream (for treatment)
- Poison ivy soap
- Powdered sports drinks mix or electrolyte additives
- Sling
- Snakebite kit
- Thermometer
- Tweezers (your multi-purpose tool may have this allowing you to dispense with it)
- Water purification tablets

If infants are with you, be sure to also carry teething ointment (such as Orajel) and diaper rash treatment.

Many of the items should be taken out of their store packaging to make placement in your fanny pack or backpack easier. In addition, small amounts of some items – such as baking soda and cotton swabs – can be placed inside re-sealable plastic bags, since you won't need the whole amount purchased.

Make sure the first-aid items are in a waterproof container. A re-sealable plastic zipper bag is perfectly fine. As Washburn County sports a humid climate, be sure to replace the adhesive bandages every couple of months, as they can deteriorate in the moistness. Also, check your first-aid kit every few trips and after any hike in which you've just used it, so that you can replace used components and to make sure medicines haven't expired.

If you have older elementary-age kids and teenagers who've been trained in first aid, giving them a kit to carry as well as yourself is a good idea. Should they find themselves lost or if you cannot get to them for a few moments, the kids might need to provide very basic first aid to one another.

Hiking with Children: Attitude Adjustment

To enjoy hiking with kids, you'll first have to adopt your child's perspective. Simply put, we must learn to hike on our kids' schedules – even though they may not know that's what we're doing.

Compared to adults, kids can't walk as far, they can't walk as fast, and they will grow bored more quickly. Every step we take requires three for them. In addition, early walkers, up to two years of age, prefer to wander than to "hike." Preschool kids will start to walk the trail, but at a rate of only about a mile per hour. With stops, that can turn a three-mile hike into a four-hour journey. Kids also won't be able to hike as steep of trails as you or handle as inclement of weather as you might.

This all may sound limiting, especially to long-time backpackers used to racking up miles or bagging peaks on their hikes, but it's really not. While you may have to put off some backcountry and mountain climbing trips for a while, it also opens up to you a number of great short trails and nature hikes with spectacular sights that you may have otherwise skipped because they weren't challenging enough.

So sure, you'll have to make some compromises, but the payout is high. You're not personally on the hike to get a workout but to spend quality time with your children.

Family Dog

Dogs are part of the family, and if you have children, they'll want to share the hiking experience with their pets. In turn, dogs will have a blast on the trail, some larger dogs can be used as Sherpas, and others will defend against threatening animals.

But there is a downside to dogs. Many will chase animals and so run the risk of getting lost or injured. Also, a doggy bag will have to be carried for dog pooh – yeah, it's natural, but also inconsiderate to leave for other hikers to smell and for their kids to step in. In addition, most dogs almost always will lose a battle against a threatening animal, so there's a price to be paid for your safety.

Many places where you'll hike solve the dilemma for you as dogs aren't allowed on their trails. Dogs are verboten on some Wisconsin state parks trails but usually permitted on those in national forests. Always check with the park ranger before heading to the trail.

If you can bring a dog, make sure it is well behaved and friendly to others. You don't need your dog biting another hiker while unnecessarily defending its family.

Rules of the Trail

Ah, the woods or a wide open meadow, peaceful and quiet, not a single soul around for miles. Now you and your children can do whatever you want.

Not so fast.

Act like wild animals on a hike, and you'll destroy the very aspects of the wilds that make them so attractive. You're also likely to end up back in civilization, specifically an emergency room. And there are other people around. Just as you would wish them to treat you courteously, so you and your children should do the same for them.

Let's cover how to act civilized out in the wilds.

Minimize damage to your surroundings

When on the trail, follow the maxim of "Leave no trace." Obviously, you shouldn't toss litter on the ground, start rock-slides, or pollute water supplies. How much is damage and how much is good-natured exploring is a gray area, of course. Most serious backpackers will say you should never pick up objects, break branches, throw rocks, pick flowers, and so on – the idea is not to disturb the environment at all.

Good luck getting a four-year-old to think like that. The good news is a four-year-old won't be able to throw around many rocks or break many branches.

Still, children from their first hike into the wilderness should be taught to respect nature and to not destroy their environment. While you might overlook a preschooler hurling rocks into a puddle, they can be taught to sniff rather than pick flowers. As they grow older, you can teach them the value of leaving the rock alone. Regardless of age, don't allow children to write on boulders or carve into trees.

Many hikers split over picking berries. To strictly abide by the "minimize damage" principle, you wouldn't pick any berries at all. Kids, however, are likely to find great pleasure in eating blackberries, currants and thimbleberries as ambling down the trail. Personally, I don't see any problem enjoying a few berries if the long-term payoff is a respect and love for nature. To minimize damage, teach them to only pick berries they can reach from the trail so they don't trample plants or deplete food supplies for animals. They also should only pick what they'll eat.

Collecting is another issue. In national and most state and county parks, taking rocks, flower blossoms and even pine cones is illegal. Picking flowers moves many species, especially if they are rare and native, one step closer to extinction. Archeological ruins are extremely fragile, and even touching them can damage a site.

But on many trails, especially gem trails, collecting is part of the adventure. Use common sense – if the point of the trail is to find materials to collect, such as a gem trail, take judiciously, meaning don't overcollect. Otherwise, leave it there.

Sometimes the trail crosses private land. If so, walking around fields, not through them, always is best or you could damage a farmer's crops.

Pack out what you pack in

Set the example as a parent: Don't litter yourself; whenever stopping, pick up whatever you've dropped; and always require kids to pick up after themselves when they litter. In the spirit of "Leave no trace," try to leave the trail cleaner than you found it, so if you come across litter that's safe to pick up, do so and bring it back to a trash bin in civilization. Given this, you may want to bring a plastic bag to carry out garbage.

Picking up litter doesn't just mean gum and candy wrappers but also some organic materials that take a long time to decompose and aren't likely to be part of the natural environment you're hiking. In particular, these include peanut shells, orange peelings, and eggshells.

Burying litter, by the way, isn't viable. Either animals or erosion soon will dig it up, leaving it scattered around the trail and woods.

Stay on the trail

Hiking off trail means potentially damaging fragile growth. Following this rule not only ensures you minimize damage but is also a matter of safety. Off trail is where kids most likely will encounter dangerous animals and poisonous plants. Not being able to see where they're stepping also increases the likelihood of falling and injuring themselves. Leaving the trail raises the chances of getting lost. Staying on the trail also means staying out of caves, mines or abandoned structures you may encounter. They are usually dangerous places.

Finally, never let children take a shortcut on a switchback trail. Besides putting them on steep ground upon which they could slip, their impatient act will cause the switchback to erode.

Trail Dangers

On Washburn County trails, two common dangers face hikers: ticks and poison ivy/sumac. Both can make miserable your time on the trail or once back home. Fortunately, both threats are easily avoidable and treatable.

Ticks

One of the greatest dangers comes from the smallest of creatures: ticks. Both the wood and the deer tick are common in Washburn County and can infect people with Lyme disease.

Ticks usually leap onto people from the top of a grass blade as you brush against it, so walking in the middle of the trail away from high plants is a good idea. Wearing a hat, a long sleeve shirt tucked into pants, and pants tucked into shoes or socks, also will keep ticks off you, though this is not foolproof as they sometimes can hook onto clothing. A tightly woven cloth provides the best protection, however. Children can pick up a tick that has hitchhiked onto the family dog, so outfit Rover and Queenie with a tick-repelling collar.

After hiking into an area where ticks live, you'll want to examine your children's bodies (as well as your own) for them. Check warm, moist areas of the skin, such as under the arms, the groin and head hair. Wearing light-colored clothing helps make the tiny tick easier to spot.

To get rid of a tick that has bitten your child, drip either disinfectant or rubbing alcohol on the bug, so it will loosen its grip. Grip the tick close to its head, slowly pulling it away from the skin. This hopefully will prevent it from releasing saliva that spreads disease. Rather than kill the tick, keep it in a plastic bag so that medical professionals can analyze it should disease symptoms appear. Next, wash the bite area with soap and water then apply antiseptic.

In the days after leaving the woods, also check for signs of disease from ticks. Look for bulls-eye rings, a sign of a Lyme disease. Other symptoms include a large red rash, joint pain, and flu-like symptoms. Indications of Rocky Mountain spotted fever include headache, fever, severe muscle aches, and a spotty rash first on palms and feet soles that spread, all beginning about two days after the bite.

If any of these symptoms appear, seek medical attention immediately. Fortunately, antibiotics exist to cure most tick-related diseases.

Poison ivy/sumac

Often the greatest danger in the wilds isn't our own clumsiness or foolhardiness but various plants we encounter. The good news is that we mostly have to force the encounter with flora. Touching the leaves of either poison ivy or poison sumac in particular results in an itchy, painful rash. Each plant's sticky resin, which causes the reaction, clings to clothing and hair, so you may not have "touched" a leaf, but once your hand runs against the resin on shirt or jeans, you'll probably get the rash.

To avoid touching these plants, you'll need to be able to identify each one. Remember the "Leaves of three, let it be" rule for poison ivy. Besides groups of three leaflets, poison ivy has shiny green leaves that are red in spring and fall. Poison sumac's leaves are not toothed as are non-poisonous sumac, and in autumn their leaves turn scarlet. Be forewarned that even after leaves fall off, poison oak's stems can carry some of the itchy resin.

By staying on the trail and walking down its middle rather than the edges, you are unlikely to come into contact with this pair of irritating plants. That probably is the best preventative. Poison ivy barrier creams also can be helpful, but they only temporarily block the resin. This lulls you into a false sense of safety, and so you may not bother to watch for poison ivy.

To treat poison ivy/sumac, wash the part of the body that has touched the plant with poison ivy soap and cold water. This will erode the oily resin, so it'll be easier to rinse off. If you don't have any of this special soap, plain soap sometimes will work if used within a half-hour of touching the plant. Apply a poison ivy cream and get medical attention immediately. Wearing gloves, remove any clothing (including shoes) that has touched the plants, washing them and the worn gloves right away.

For more about these topics and many others, pick up this author's "Hikes with Tykes: A Practical Guide to Day Hiking with Kids." You also can find tips online at the author's "Day Hiking Trails" blog. Have fun on the trail!

Index

About the Author

Rob Bignell is a long-time hiker, editor, and author of the popular "Hikes with Tykes," "Headin' to the Cabin," "Hittin' the Trail," and "Best Sights to See" guidebooks and several other titles. He and his son Kieran have been hiking together for the past decade. Rob has served as an infantryman in the Army National Guard and taught middle school students in New Mexico and Wisconsin. His newspaper work has won several national and state journalism awards, from editorial writing to sports reporting. In 2001, The Prescott Journal, which he served as managing editor of, was named Wisconsin's Weekly Newspaper of the Year. Rob and Kieran live in Wisconsin.

CHECK OUT THESE OTHER HIKING BOOKS BY ROB BIGNELL

"Hikes with Tykes" series:
- Hikes with Tykes: A Practical Guide to Day Hiking with Children
- Hikes with Tykes: Games and Activities

"Headin' to the Cabin" series:
- Day Hiking Trails of Northwest Wisconsin
- Day Hiking Trails of Northeast Minnesota

"Hittin' the Trail" series:

National parks
- Best Sights to See at America's National Parks
- Great Smoky Mountain National Park
- Grand Canyon National Park (ebook only)

Minnesota
- Gooseberry Falls State Park

Minnesota/Wisconsin
- Interstate State Park
- St. Croix National Scenic Riverway

Wisconsin
- Barron County
- Bayfield County
- Burnett County (ebook only)
- Chippewa Valley (Eau Claire, Chippewa, Dunn, Pepin counties)
- Crex Meadows Wildlife Area (ebook only)
- Douglas County
- Polk County
- Sawyer County

GET CONNECTED!

Follow the author to learn about other great trails and for useful hiking tips:

- Blog: *hikeswithtykes.blogspot.com*
- Facebook: *dld.bz/fBq2C*
- Google+: *dld.bz/fBq2s*
- LinkedIn: *linkedin.com/in/robbignell*
- Pinterest: *pinterest.com/rbignell41*
- Twitter: *twitter.com/dayhikingtrails*
- Website: *dayhikingtrails.wordpress.com*

www.ingramcontent.com/pod-product-compliance
Lightning Source LLC
Chambersburg PA
CBHW050542280326
41933CB00011B/1687